SECOND SERIES

More Classics to Moderns

Compiled and edited by Denes Agay

It is with pleasure that we present More Classics To Moderns. It is a sequel to our now widely used Classics To Moderns.

Because of the extended period of music history in both books, beginning pianists of all ages will discover material well suited to their needs. This material is easy enough to be used by the beginning student as his first sight reading book. At the university level, the student will find a rich source of reference to supplement his study of theory and composition.

The original compositions selected by Denes Agay involved extensive research covering the piano literature of more than three centuries. There is a wide representation of composers, including some of the lesser known masters, all of whom the player will be delighted to encounter.

All selections are in their original form, neither re-arranged nor simplified. They appear in approximately chronological order. Marks of phrasing and expression are often editorial additions, especially in the music of the pre-classic period. These signs were added for a quicker and easier understanding of the structure and mood of the compositions. They are to be considered as suggestions rather than rigid directions.

Students, teachers and all pianists will find these original miniatures valuable for study, recital, sight reading or just relaxing musical entertainment of the highest calibre. *The Publishers*

Yorktown Music Press

London/New York/Sydney

Exclusive distributors:
Music Sales Limited
8/9 Frith Street, London W1V 5TZ, England
Music Sales Pty. Limited,
120 Rothschild Avenue, Rosebery, NSW 2018, Australia.
Music Sales Corporation
257 Park Avenue South, New York, NY10010, U.S.A.

This book © Copyright 1979 by
Yorktown Music Press
ISBN 0.86001.680.3
Order No. YK 20154

Music Sales complete catalogue lists thousands of titles
and is free from your local music book shop, or direct from
Music Sales Limited. Please send a cheque/postal order
for £1.50 for postage to
Music Sales Limited, 8/9 Frith Street, London W1V 5TZ

CONTENTS

Praeludium

from *The Well-Tempered Clavier, Book 1*

Johann Sebastian Bach
(1685-1750)

Allegro (♩=112)

Intrada

George Frideric Handel
(1685-1759)

Little Fugue

Domenico Zipoli
(1675-1726)

Tambourin

Jean Philippe Rameau
(1683-1764)

Andante Grazioso

Joseph Haydn
(1732–1809)

Allegro Scherzando

Joseph Haydn

Rondo
(K.15hh)

Wolfgang Amadeus Mozart
(1756–1791)

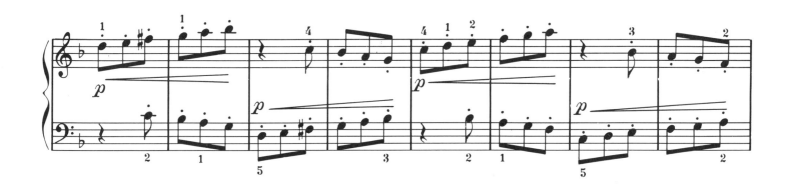

* *Small notes are editorial additions and may be omitted.*

Four Ecossaises

Ludwig van Beethoven
(1770-1827)

3.

4.

Three Waltzes

Franz Schubert
(1797-1828)

3.

At the Fireside

Op.15, No.8

Robert Schumann
(1810–1856)

Harvest Song
Op.68, No.24

Robert Schumann

Lively
with cheerful expression

mf

Interlude

César Franck
(1822–1890)

Quasi andante

Mazurka

Op.67, No.3

Frédéric Chopin
(1810–1849)

Chanson Triste

Op.40, No.2

Peter I. Tchaikovsky
(1840–1893)

Moderato con moto
la melodia con molto espressione

24

Toccatina
from Op.27

Dmitri Kabalevsky
(1904-   )

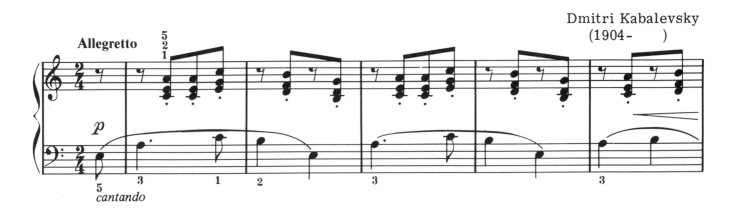

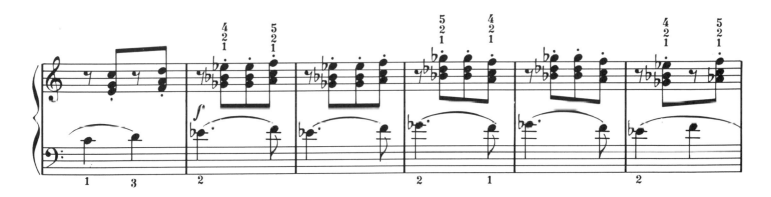

Idylle

for Debussy, from *Next-to-last Thoughts*

Eric Satie
(1866–1925)

Moderately, I beg you

What do I see?   The brook is all wet;

Basso legato, don't you think?

and the wood dry and flammable as a switch.

But my heart is

very small.   The trees look like great ill-formed combs;

On The Playground

Nikolai Rakov
(1908-   )

Brazilian Children's Song

"Farmers Daughters" from *Guia Prático*

Heitor Villa-Lobos
(1881-1959)

Printed by Printwise (Haverhill) Limited, Suffolk 12/07 (64440)